THE
Black Father
PERSPECTIVE
VOLUME 2

What We Want America to Know

COMPILED BY
KIMMOLY K. LABOO

©Copyright 2021 Kimmoly K. LaBoo

All rights reserved. This book is protected under the copyright laws of the United States of America.

ISBN-13: 978-1-954609-14-3

No portion of this book may be reproduced, distributed, or transmitted in any form, including photocopying, recording, or other electronic or mechanical methods, without the written permission of the publisher, except in the case of brief quotations embodied in reviews and certain other non-commercial uses permitted by copyright law. Permission granted on request.

For information regarding special discounts for bulk purchases, please contact the publisher: LaBoo Publishing Enterprise, LLC
staff@laboopublishing.com
www.laboopublishing.com

Scripture quotations marked (NLT) are taken from the Holy Bible, New Living Translation, copyright ©1996, 2004, 2015 by Tyndale House Foundation. Used by permission of Tyndale House Publishers, Inc., Carol Stream, Illinois 60188. All rights reserved.

Scripture quotations marked (NIV) are taken from the Holy Bible, New International Version®, NIV®. Copyright © 1973, 1978, 1984, 2011 by Biblica, Inc.™ Used by permission of Zondervan. All rights reserved worldwide. www.zondervan.com

The Holy Bible, King James Version. Cambridge Edition: 1769; *King James Bible Online*, 2019. www.kingjamesbibleonline.org.

Scripture quotations marked ESV are from the Holy Bible, English Standard Version, copyright © 2001 by Crossway Bibles, a publishing ministry of Good News Publishers. Used by permission. All rights reserved.

Table of Contents

Introduction v

More of Myself: Trevon Mosby. 1

Abandonment Syndrome – The Sense of Feeling Forgotten: Nathaniel K. Harris 13

When All You Have to Offer is Love: Jonathan E. Rudd, Sr. . . . 25

Life Keeps Life-ing: Jonathan Rudd, II 31

The Minority Struggle of America: Floyd Brown II 41

About the Visionary Author 55

Introduction

The Black Father Perspective has provided a unique opportunity to hear what is on the hearts and minds of black fathers in America. In volume I the writers showed the pure love that black men have for their children. In Vol. II the writers have given us a glimpse of their struggles, heartache, determination and perseverance. My vision for this work was to dispel myths and counter negative stereotypes regarding black men, allowing readers to experience more than what they see on the nightly news. In fact, the fathers in volume I were able to interrupt the negativity when they appeared on WMAR2, Baltimore's 11 O'clock news, showcasing the strength and love of the black father.

The work continues.

Trevon Mosby is the father of two beautiful babies. Originally from Harrisburg, Pennsylvania, he married at the age of 24 in his wife's hometown, Detroit, Michigan. Fatherhood followed shortly after and has kept him learning and evolving at an expedited rate.

Trevon attended both Bloomsburg University of Pennsylvania and Cornerstone University of Grand Rapids, Michigan. He has yet to complete his Ministry and Creative Writing degrees, but he continues to invest in his education by reading and sharpening his skills via Skillshare classes.

Fatherhood has forced Trevon to reconcile who he is with who his loved ones expect him to be. This has made for a trying two years of raising babies. As his children grow, he grows with them, being sharpened by his experiences as he settles into manhood.

Being a father and a husband are two big dreams Trevon has realized. He serves GOD and his family by living a lesson he learned from Jesus Christ: Show up, engage, and invest.

More of Myself

Trevon Mosby

• • • • • • • • • • • • •

My Heavenly Father is the only leadership I've had in my life. My dad never showed up for me. He rarely engaged with me. More rarely would he invest in me. This convinced me that he does not love me. So I decided to live my life without him, honoring and loving him without any sort of contact.

For most of my years, I've been deeply wounded, starting with my dad's absence. That first loss of emotional security shattered me before I knew what emotions were. As I matured, every way that I was failed by those I loved reminded me of what that first deep wound taught me: I am not valuable to anyone. I am not loved, seen, heard, or respected. No one will stay by my side. I am not worthy of GOD's love. I have no one to protect me from emotional harm – the strikes that could cripple me or break me entirely.

Bearing the agonizing weight of these sobering beliefs, my first ten years of life were horrifying, discouraging, and miserable. Nightmares shook me awake in my dark bedroom and the lasting terror kept me paralyzed and alert. My kindness was the first gift I gave to everyone I came in contact with; it was consistently met with confusion, fear, insult, or silence. I began believing that the love I gave was threatening – an annoyance and a disturbance of inner peace and joy. So I retreated inward.

I've been hurt for so long and no one sees my wounds. No one hears me when I cry. No one wants to help me heal. No one will save me from this Hell, I thought.

The sadness that settled in and had yet to be resolved evolved into despair. I didn't understand why I felt this way or why I believed that I might as well get comfortable in my despair or just accept what value-less trash like me does: die. Why didn't anyone want to help me? Why was I both wounded and alone? I didn't have the answers. And the silence formed a growing, burning anger in me.

I've always deeply connected with two characters: the Hulk and Wolverine. Rage fuels both of them to act in ways that often protect their world from evil that would otherwise be far-reaching. These characters are recognized as heroes for this.

I admired their heroism, the sacrifices they made to secure safety for others. They knew better than most people how it feels to be hurt and scarred – broken in places that you can't easily locate within, let alone heal from. I did too.

I decided to be the hero in my world, sacrificing my time and energy to hear people's troubles, to help others through their pain, to do for them what was never done for me: save them from suffering. I committed to being a friend to all and a hero to those who chose to hold me close.

To many of my loved ones, I may now look like the villain because of what I do and how I move to protect my babies. I won't allow selfishness near them. I don't tolerate deception or mess. The traumas that plagued me have no place in their lives, so anyone who is too proud or too hurt to do right by my babies remains far from them. A villain doesn't make you feel good – they scare you, make you uncomfortable with their words and actions. But every villain is the hero of their own story.

There's truth to the statement, "You either die a hero or you live long enough to see yourself become the villain." Like The Dark Knight, I accepted blame for the chaos and damage that ensued in my life. Relating further, I endured devastating blows in my desperate efforts to save everyone, living like I owed Man everything I had. I recently retired my cape.

Daily, dads are under the pressure of non-stop demands: Go to work. Feed your family. Help with the house. Be a paragon for your kids. Bring order to your household. Bring discipline. Get the money to move your family forward. Eat right. Sleep well. Wake up and play with your kids. Make time for your woman. Don't stop praying for your family. Don't forget about your other family members. Be there for your siblings, friends, and parents. Keep yourself in shape. Drive carefully. Don't overwhelm yourself; don't you dare lose your cool. If we fail at any of these, the consequences that follow are what threaten to push us off the edge we practically live on.

Keeping up with the growing list of needs of everyone who is important to you weakens your strength to get it all done, to be the man and play the role of leader in your family. But in your kids' eyes, you never lose that strength. As long as you show up, you are someone's hero. So you can retire your cape too, but you will always be someone's hero and it won't be too long before you're called into action again.

Some say when you have children, you become more of yourself. I deny myself the right to be vulnerable – because it almost always leads to immense hurt and overwhelming disappointment. I deny myself the right to rest – because I recognize my loved ones' pleas for my time, energy, and attention. I've been criticized for staying to myself, villainized for minding my business and not being too concerned about what's going wrong for everyone. Saving others and being a hero to myself were two demands of my character that began to clash. My story was confronting me, forcing me (to this day) to change as my wife and I anticipated the births of our babies. So far, their lives have meant for me that I'm always declaring who I am through my decisions, which primarily show my children who I want to be and how their world is shaped.

When my son was born, I felt so cast aside by medical staff that I was numb to the birth our second child. While I was the most important presence in the room for my wife, I was a nearly non-existent, unnecessary puzzle piece to my family according to the statistics that were shared with us at the hospital. The world has accepted the reality of absent fathers as a faithful truth and because it was faithful to me, I've become even more committed to ending the cycle. I knew thoroughly what my failure could do to my babies.

Being a "9-5 dad" was never in my plan. Working so often during the first years of my children's lives makes me feel like I actually am absent in my home. I miss out on a lot of their milestones: my daughter's new words, my son's abilities to sit up and roll over. They're growing so fast and I'm not present to witness those precious moments in their development. Every day that I am with them, time flies by so quickly. I know I'll never be able to make up for the time together that we're losing. My life-long dream of being a father was crushed as I slowly realized that this may be the first and deepest wound my children would need help recovering from. I've experienced their excitement when I come through our front door. I've seen their expectant, saddening faces as the door closes behind me – even if I'm just taking out the trash. I won't forget my daughter's heartbroken wails when I'd come home from working 12-hour overnight shifts and had to run to the bathroom instead of greeting her first.

Parenting has shown me how wonderful it is to be missed – to be loved, not because you fulfill a role, or fill a void, but because your consistency created trust. Your attention and love are appreciated. Being a Black father – one plagued by generations of trauma as well as unhealed and pried-open wounds, one who is encouraged to live fearfully with all the eggshells other traumatized people placed around me – it's the scariest reality to live.

My babies are among the number that see it. They feel how this world afflicts me and I love them for it. Without a child's love, a man may lose his inner child, that sacred place where peace, joy, and love begin. Someone's got to love you just because they love you. No reason. No criteria you're meeting in their mind. No unspoken give-and-take deals. Just pure love. A man has a need to be seen, heard, and adored while completely exposed, vulnerable to words and energy. My babies satisfy these needs – as often as I let them. They're eager to give love and I'm almost always just as eager to receive it and give my own.

Fatherhood comes with great expectations, which makes it easy to fail, and just as easy or nearly impossible to triumph. These expectations are the obstacles that can make us feel like everything we hold close to our hearts is closing in on us and there's no way of escape. This is what I saw for the first eighteen months of being a father. I worked one job that nearly broke my body. I worked another that exhausted my help. I worked another that threatened my own health and the well-being of my family. Overworked and stressed beyond what I could handle, a break never materialized. Providing for his family is among the most important tasks a man is assigned when he makes children. I have no other option but to suit up and show up to get the job done.

A man under pressure makes for a strong image and a bleeding bearer or a living, bleeding portrait. Providing, leading, and protecting require your best efforts. That blood, that sweat, and those tears are shed from the pain we endure from some of our worst experiences that empowered us to step into our positions of leadership in the first place. Whether we suffer in silence or are transparent with our babies, our best never goes unnoticed.

My coworker asks me all the time, "How is your family?" "Happy, healthy, and growing" is what I tell him every time. And I want that to be true for us, always. The hero in me wants to save my entire world: every friend I have, every friend of my wife, every family member our children can claim. What I'm coming to understand is that as I present lasting peace to my household, everyone that we love beyond our four walls can choose to participate in the peace we establish and choose. Those may sound like villainous words to those who value family and bloodlines and childhood memories. But those words sound like the inner peace of a people that continues to evolve beyond trauma, unforgiveness, and patterns of woundedness.

Perfection can never be credited to humanity. However, effort can be. I can try my best to be what you want or need me to be and one thing is going to happen, with two consequences. In my eyes, I will have died trying. In your eyes, I will have died failing to fully understand and meet your needs. The hero in me has to die and I must carry on having faith that my world is already saved and there's no need to repeat JESUS' sacrifice for "my people." Those who perceive me to be a villain are responsible for how they see me. They must carry on with the burden of understanding or the lack of it. My focus can then be on the life of emotional safety, spiritual and physical security, and mental freedom that I am building with my wife for our family. We intend to send each of our children on their own way as adults without the scars and misinformation that we inherited. Parents, our children do not have to carry the full burden of our heartbreaking history. Know that doing your best will get them far from repeating what traumas already plague their DNA. Furthermore, please trust that you doing GOD's best – parenting as you are led by HIS Perfect example – is what will lead them farther away from familiar pains.

I never asked my dad to be my hero or to get everything right as a seventeen-year-old new father. In my own babies' infancy, I see clearly that a new life you brought into this world – a new life that echoes the best and worst of who you are – obliviously asks you to simply be around them and to try being their parent. There is no manual to parenthood and so-called expert parents are no experts of how to parent your kid(s). As a dad, you get to nurture a part of you from the moment they emerge from the womb to the final moments of their childhood when you trust them to endure the consequences of their own decisions and go on nurturing the person you love. Your child is asking you to show up for their triumphs and for their griefs. Show up on the paths they choose and in the moments they feel lost. They're asking you to engage with them as best you can. You don't need the perfect words for them and you don't need an answer for every comment or question. Invest your wisdom and emotions into your children. You never know what your investment will return to you through the life of your baby.

I am a young father with few informing stories about my kids. But my hopes for their lives are rich and vast. As a younger man, I dreamt of having children of my own to give my abundance of love to, to share wisdom with and to learn from. I've always wanted to serve GOD by being the present, attentive, wise, nurturing, sacrificing leader my children would need me to be. I am so blessed to say that I see the good fruit of pursuing this dream when I experience my children.

What I can offer to other young fathers like me is this: Pay attention to what stresses you out and if it cannot be removed from your life, address it with patience after you've given yourself a break from it. It's so easy to succumb to all the crying, diaper changing, demands to play, and being woken up to meet the needs of your babies. It's exhausting work being a dad. That work does not stop when your plate is full or when you're spent from dealing with any- and everything else. At one point, all of this changed my perspective on life as I was living it. I saw most things through the lens of frustration, desperate to know when I would be able to sleep again and spend time alone with my wife. When would I get some peace?

The more I begged that question, the more trauma would answer me. In the midst of these most stressful moments in my fatherhood journey, life-long fears that were once too great for me to fully grasp became abundantly clear to me as I realized I still held tight to them. Some of the family members that consistently devastated me emotionally came to me with anger and expectations that triggered some bold, honest reactions from me. As the dust settled, I learned that childhood trauma will continue to resurface and pull you backwards if you continue to react to it. Trauma requires a response, not a reaction. When a man responds to a problem, it can finally be resolved: The problem loses the power you gave it when you reacted to it. Your peace must be built, and the decisions you make are both the foundation and the structure of it. Every person is the product of their experiences and their responses to them. If you have yet to respond to the painful, toxic areas of your life, the structure of your peace will be weak and the foundation unstable.

Failing to confront your fears when they attack you can create a cycle of instability for your children. On some days, you may be joyful and playful. On others, you may be a hair's breadth away from a meltdown that could scar them for the majority of their lives. Joy and pain are promised in the lives we live, but as we mature, we have to decide which will be more consistent – especially when other lives depend on how you live yours.

Our babies are human beings, experiencing the world for the first time with as much knowledge of it as the shared experience that you and your woman grant them. Before they know GOD, our Creator, they will know you. They will rely on you for the truth and protection as they learn and grow. Their morality will be formed by the experiences they have with you. Every lesson they learn will be challenged by the lessons they were taught by you.

To my disbelief, I've witnessed parents wield the responsibilities of parenthood against the babies they raised. The position gave them power they never had, so that power was misused in ways that paralyzed some of their children, sabotaged others, and destroyed the relationships that they could have with their parents as adults. When you remain in pain, you bleed onto the people who value you and more often than not, you're not aware of how you're hurting them, of how you're influencing them to make choices that they hope will make the bleeding stop.

Commit daily to healing, fathers. Surround yourself with people you trust and help that sees you situated in the peace you're building. Protect your peace by any means necessary. Family and friends are no exceptions to the way you want to live your life. The power you discover on your healing journey will show your little humans the power that they have, leading them to walk in the strength, growing wisdom, and confidence of their fathers.

"There's so much negative imagery of black fatherhood. I've got tons of friends that are doing the right thing by their kids, and doing the right thing as a father — and how come that's not as newsworthy?"

Will Smith

Nathaniel K. Harris, Sr. can best be described as a man of great faith in God. Devoted to being a great father, he is focused on being an influence and role model to his four children. He is a published author, full-time employee, musician, athletic coach and mentor.

Nathaniel is currently attending Regent University pursuing a Bachelor of Arts degree in Biblical and Theological studies. One of the greatest things that Nathaniel has is a great imagination. Writing has been one of the ways he has learned to cope with any issue that he has been faced with. He enjoys creating opportunities to make those around him smile because of what he has said or done.

Abandonment Syndrome – The Sense of Feeling Forgotten

"Just Being There!"

Nathaniel K. Harris

• • • • • • • • • • • • •

Where is everyone? That is the question that most people ask when they feel alone or abandoned. Countless people have a sense of abandonment, especially when they feel or even believe that no one cares about them. What is interesting is that most people have not dealt with the issues of their past and feel the need of affirmation that they are not left alone or forgotten about. As black fathers, we have an awesome task ahead of us. We have the stereotype against us. We have the weight of the family—the need to provide and protect. Most importantly, most have children who look up to us and are watching to see how we handle a crisis. In this chapter, I want to look at some of the issues that we face as black men. I want to identify the abandonment syndrome and the sense of being forgotten. In the end, I want to highlight the importance of "Just Being There!"

As I considered this topic, I was reminded of the Lenten Season message of the historic utterances of Jesus. The scripture states that as Jesus was hanging on the cross, He cried with a loud voice, "Eli, Eli, lama sabachthani?" That is simply asking, "My God, my God, why hast thou forsaken me?" Matthew 27:46, KJV. William MacDonald shares that the Lord Jesus had no sin of His own but took the guilt of sin upon Himself. When God, as judge, looked down and saw our sins upon the sinless substitute, He withdrew from the Son of His love.

There is a great possibility that most people have felt rejected or even neglected at some point. Even as we reflect on this scripture, we witness our loving Savior at His most vulnerable state, wondering if the Father in heaven has forgotten about Him. We, as believers, are not exempt from the abandonment feeling. As we have read in the scriptural text, even Christ found the need to ask if God was going to help.

The gift that most fathers can have is to create and father children. There are some who have abandoned that responsibility and have caused others to shoulder the responsibility of the parent. One of the most disappointing bits of news that you can hear is when there are children who are wondering where their fathers are and why they do not want to spend time with them. The topic of being a deadbeat father quite honestly bothers me because there are some that have never supported their children and totally reject the child because of the uncomfortable relationship with the child's other parent.

In my personal life, I have been accused of not being a part of my older children's life; I was accused of being an absentee father. In other words, it would suggest that I am a deadbeat father. With my older children living in another state, it is a four-hour drive to visit. In all stretches of the imagination, seeing my oldest children was only done as a planned vacation trip. There was a lot of planning and coordinating that was involved with making the visit possible.

There was a conversation that I had with my daughter that I seem to give my youngest children more attention than I have ever given them. What was relayed to me was that, as a father, I am not being fair with all of my children. It was the assumption that I abandoned the oldest children and rejected them. In reality, the younger children seemed to have reaped the better benefit of me because I was with them while the oldest were living in another state over 277 miles away.

My heart goes out to the young sons and daughters who do not have their parents, especially their fathers. The concern is what their aspirations are and what they will gravitate to as a lifestyle. Often, we see the young black brothers and sisters on the street corners who are suspiciously looking to cop customers for supposed drug sales. When you see this, you can see the pain of wanting to survive and the need to feel wanted. These young brothers and sisters are in the streets looking to get money only to look good on the surface. Most of these young people are only interested in making enough money to purchase the latest tennis shoes and clothes. It appears that these young people are only in the entry level position because of the missing component of an influential, positive role model. In most cases, these people are shown love and a false sense of security when the older people promise them street love.

As I have stated, I am adamant about assuring my children that I will always be there, and I made it a point to make sure I pick them up from school. There was a time that the school that my sons attended had a tough time controlling their dismissal program. Most of the time, there was a line from the school trailing for blocks. It was nothing to be in a waiting line for at least thirty-five minutes.

One particular day, I was delayed at work to complete an assignment. This caused me to leave work a little later than I normally would. With that, I figured I had plenty of time because the line for dismissal would be long and I would have plenty of time to pick him up. When I finally left work, I was sure that I was still in a place to pick my son up from school without him even knowing that I was late.

When I arrived at the school, I was truly shocked to see that there was not one car waiting to pick up children for dismissal. My concern was where was my son and where did he wander off to? To make this moment worse, I was able to park directly in front of the school building and there was no sign of teachers or my son. I parked my car and hurried into the school building to see where my son was. When I walked in, a teacher greeted me, asked me who I was and shared that the children who were left were taken to the auditorium to await their pickup.

As I turned the corner to the auditorium, I noticed my son in tears, as if something bad happened. For almost ten minutes, I continued to ask him why he was crying and why he was so upset. After he calmed down, he looked at me and said he was scared because I wasn't there at my normal time to pick him up. He also shared that he was afraid something bad happened to me. But the thing that he said next made tears come to my eyes. He stated that he thought that I had forgotten about him. The pain in those words caused both of us to start crying. At that point, I had to affirm that I would never forget about him and the only reason that I was late was because I needed to finish something at work. To this day, I make sure that I never miss a pickup time unless I have made arrangements with my wife or someone else to pick them up.

As a father, I found it vitally important that people saw a black father's presence at the school my sons were attending. After we transferred both of my younger sons to another school, I wanted to make sure that the teachers and other parents knew that these boys had a father in their life. One particular dismissal, I was in the area where both of my sons were to be dismissed. It appeared that the entire school dismissed at the exact same time. My youngest son's class was running late so I went to meet up with my other son. While I was heading toward him, I noticed an older boy talking to my son. I did recognize that my sons make friends easily so the age difference did not bother me. But as I got closer, I saw my son's gesture toward him and I heard him say, "Naw, I'm good!"

As I reached him, I pressured him to tell me what the boy asked him. He was reluctant to tell me but I do believe that he saw the father-fire in my eyes. He looked at me and shared that the boy asked him if he wanted to be in his gang. Needless to say, I walked back up to the school to confront the boy. Here we had an older middle school boy asking my elementary school-aged son to be in a gang. I never saw the boy that day, but I did make the principal and the teachers aware that the middle school boy proposed a gang membership to my son and I would not accept that. By fate, the nightly news aired a segment that gang recruitment was being entertained even as early as elementary school. This caused me to sit down with the youngest two children to share the dangers of gang affiliation and the importance of watching each other's back and watching their surroundings.

As a father, there are many situations that can be considered as Screen Door Moments. What does that mean? In one of our men's small group meetings, we were introduced to a story that shared the disappointment of a son to his father. The story is shared that over a period of time, the son was being bullied and harassed. Possibly because the bully was bigger, he would run home every day and lock the door. This routine was repeated every day after school, which caused the father to ask about it in concern. When asked, the son just replied that there was nothing wrong.

One day, the curious father decided to stand by the door exactly at the time the boy would arrive home from school. Just like clockwork, he noticed his son running up the street. Instead of waiting for the reasoning, he decided to teach his son a lesson. When the son went to open the door, he noticed that the screen door was locked. As he pulled and tugged, the door never opened. The father walked to the door, telling his son that no son of his would be a punk and run from a fight.

This put the son in an awkward position because he could not run from this bully any longer because the screen door was locked. But the other issue is that he felt that his father left him out there to fend for himself. Now I must be honest, this is troubling. You have this kid who felt that his father left him out there to possibly be slaughtered by this bully, or this could be what caused him to face his bully and fight back. The ending was never told but if I can use my imagination, I can just see this boy made to go and face this person that had been harassing him. One thing about a bully is that he loses his power when his victim stops running. I can also understand the young boy's disappointment. The person that he should be able to rely on to help in this trouble locked the screen door on him. That was his father.

In our modern society, it appears that our black and brown men have a target on their back. By default, the color of their skin can suggest to others that they are a threat. Even if they are not doing anything or causing chaos or mischief, some are labeled as monsters because of the stereotype that has been created. That means that when one person has messed up, the perception is that all are trouble. With me having one girl and three boys, I have the task of instructing my children to abide by the law as best as they can. I remind them to say 'yes ma'am and no ma'am. I even share that presenting yourself in a positive light will possibly keep the heat from you. Although that is an awesome idea, the news media has proven that has not always worked.

My oldest son is carving his way into adulthood and life. My prayer has been that God would protect him as he is living his life. My conversation with him is a bit different than those with my daughter and my youngest sons. I had to explain to him how to conduct himself at the worksite. I had to pre-warn him of the conversations that may be addressed to him because he is young and African

American. I had to remind him of his manners and how he should conduct himself in public.

What is interesting is that I had to share with him the importance of speaking as if he knew some phonics and to talk with complete sentences. In other words, not to have conversations with people as if he was texting on his cell phone. It is a horrible thought, but these days, you must remind them to pull their pants above their waist and put on a belt. The issue that is presented is that the appearance of a person can label them a target. Even more than that, sometimes, there are clothing styles and colors that would suggest that they are criminals.

Why is it so important to "just be there?" There needs to be a generation of black fathers who can stand up and provide assurance that there are some black fathers who are respectful and awesome role models. There is a great need to raise up black leaders that will be proud of the relationships that they are in and show responsibility with their children. On the nightly news, it appears that the only news that is being aired is how black males are being portrayed as criminals and animals.

It appears that most of our black males (especially) are either dying in the streets or are in the prison systems. Years ago, I was asked to be a part of a proposal that would allow our church to go into the local jail and present our ministry. After careful consideration, I asked the question "then what?" That question was posed because these young men in the prison system may feel like they have been abandoned and there may not be any hope for them if they are released. I asked what would be in place to prevent recidivism.

What would be the offer for job placement? What would be in place to serve as a better option than substance abuse? What would be in place for temporary housing and shelter?

In other words, there needs to be something in place to connect people to a life that they may never have known. Not just for the people that were locked up, but what can be put in place for people not to feel disconnected and left feeling abandoned? There are people who struggle with the abandonment syndrome. By definition, this can be described as an adverse experience that leaves a person feeling unsafe, fearful and alone. If a person is not careful, this abandonment syndrome can follow them for the rest of their life.

One suggestion to help combat this is to first recognize who God is to you. I am convinced that no issue or circumstance can be resolved without realizing that God is needed in your life. Many may not accept that statement or even agree, but the truth of the matter is that the only comfort we have is that He will never leave us. The scriptures share that after Moses died, Joshua was now tasked to take on the role as the lead pastor to the children of Israel. God admonished Joshua to be strong and courageous. *Do not be frightened, and do not be dismayed. The Lord, your God, will be with you wherever you go.* Joshua 1:9, NIV. In the areas where we feel left alone or abandoned, He will be there.

Great parenting is necessary. Children must see a nurturing mother and a providing father. Even in the society that we live in, parents must be present in the child's life. Unfortunately, we live in a society where some children live in broken homes or are subject to behaviors seen in broken relationships. For men, it is important to fight for your relationship and your children. One thing that some children struggle with is the absence of the father. As the chapter title states, the black father needs to just be there. The reality is no relationship is perfect, but the reward is maintaining a healthy relationship so that the children can identify what a relationship looks like when couples work together.

As far as feeling forgotten, some people need to be affirmed that they are not. There are some awesome peer groups that aid in getting people involved so they do not feel forgotten, but rather connected. There are hobbies and other interests that you may have, this may be the time to dust off that old dream and begin to put it in motion. Someone once asked me when I felt lonely or abandoned, what did I do? I found out that I love to be creative.

As a musician, I love creating music and sound. In my house, there is literally every instrument you can imagine. One of the gifts that I have is playing the drums. Whether on the acoustic set, electronic set or the computer sound, I love to create new ideas. Not that I have mastered any of the other instruments—it is the fact that I can make music and sounds. One thing that I am learning is that I love to write. I am creating stories and characters that parallel my life, but also encourage someone through my testimony. My word of advice is to allow the gift in you to spring forth. Everyone has a gift. Everyone has their "IT." Whenever you feel left out or abandoned, use your "IT." You will never know how much it will encourage someone else.

Just be there! Although times are rough and situations look bleak, it shows great character when a person can tighten up their boot straps and stand in the midst of calamity. There is an unfortunate stigma that suggests that black men run from their troubles and do not face them head-on. I want to speak to those men who know the power in standing. The reward for standing in crisis is the ability to build character. Although that may sound absurd, the true test of a man is to be able to shoulder the weight of life and continue show forth integrity even in tough times.

God bless!

**Jonathan E. Rudd, Sr.** is the former pastor of Living God's Word Outreach Ministries. He was married for 43 years to S. Helen Rudd until she passed away in his arms on February 7, 2018. From that union came two sons, Jonathan E. Rudd, II and Stephon D. Rudd, and he is the proud grandfather of eight grandchildren. God blessed him to find love again in the person of Benita Cheryl, and together they have begun the next chapter in his life.

He is the author of the book, "Faith That Recovers All - Taking Back What the Enemy Stole." Although raised in the church, he did not find salvation until 1974 when he attended a little church in Washington, DC. For many years he studied the Bible under the teaching of R.G. Hardy in Baltimore, MD. Before becoming a pastor, he travelled as an evangelist speaking across the country in several states including New York, New Jersey, Delaware, and many states in the south.

What he considers as his greatest accomplishment is being a husband, father, grandfather, and a friend to many. His motto in life is, "I've never met a stranger, they're just friends I'm meeting for the first time."

When All You Have to Offer is Love

Jonathan E. Rudd, Sr.

• • • • • • • • • • • • • •

The year was 1974. I was fresh out of the military after touring Germany for over two years. To be exact, it was two years, seven months, and 23 days! The Army and I were not the best of friends. They wanted me out and I wanted out. I had become a heavy drinker and a substance abuser. I was fortunate enough to get out with an honorable discharge, but it was not easy. It was the early 70s and tensions were still high from the assassination of Martin Luther King, Jr. My reaction to his death resulted in my inability to accept the idea of a white man telling me what to do.

That was before I had an experience that would change my life forever. I was angry, frustrated and as they say, mad at the world. My girlfriend dumped me without an explanation while I was in the Army, and I wanted to know why. I tried to find the courage to pick up the phone and call, but I just could not bring myself to do it. My parents were divorced (they later remarried), and my father was remarried to another woman. To top it all off, I was dating the daughter of my father's new wife, only to find out that she was my half-sister (neither of us knew about this skeleton hiding in our family's closet). Thankfully, I never got to third base before my brother told us.

I don't know if I was angrier at my father, my ex-girlfriend (the one that dumped me), or myself. That was when I sought the counsel of the wisest person I knew: my mother. Her suggestion was to go with her to church. Church? That's your advice? I had not seen the inside of a church since I was a kid; why should I go now? Reluctantly, I went with her to a little church in Washington, DC. That was where things changed for me. In my mind, I was there to find a new girlfriend, but God had other plans! I made it a point to sit as far to the back of the church as possible. This was for two reasons. First, by sitting in the back, I could scope out all the single women in the church, which was my primary goal. But the second reason for sitting in the back was to *not* get noticed by the minister of the evening. Part one of my plan worked well; I had narrowed my choices down to three potential candidates. However, part two failed miserably!

The preacher that evening, a small-framed white woman named Sister Sword, looked in my direction and called me to the front of the church. I tried to act as if I didn't know who she was pointing to, but I knew, and so did everyone else in the church. I hesitantly walked up to the front and listened to her words. "Young man, I saw a light shining over you, and I knew God was calling you." My first thought was, *This lady is crazy. A light shining on* me? *She is sadly mistaken!* Before I could finish the thought in my mind, I was laid out in the floor as if someone had knocked me in the head. I gave my life to the Lord that evening.

Why do I tell this story? It was that night that I met the mother of my two sons, Jonathan II and Stephon. Helen and I were married seven months after that night, and my first son, Jonathan II, was born 11 months later. I was a proud father, but I had no job. How could I take care of this bundle of joy without a job? I loved my son, but how could I feed and care for him without a job? You cannot feed, clothe, and shelter a child with love. You need money! We were getting by on my now wife's salary, but the bills kept mounting up faster than we could pay. I had to do something, and soon.

We had made friends with some of the church members, and one family invited us to move in with them until we got on our feet. That went well for a while, but eventually, the pressure to get our own place increased. As a man, I felt useless because I was unable to provide for my family. I told the Lord that I would do any kind of legal and honest work to provide for my newborn son and wife. God took me up on that challenge. I worked every kind of job that came my way. I mowed lawns, picked up trash, worked in corrections, drove school busses, and worked for just about every Federal Government agency that would hire me.

Blue collar, white collar, or no collar at all—if they were hiring, I was applying. We were finally able to get an apartment of our own in Columbia, MD. It wasn't much, but it was ours, and that was all that mattered. In 1978 we were able to buy our first home in Baltimore, MD. By then, my second son Stephon was in the picture. This time, however, I was better prepared. The struggles and sacrifices we made to ensure the welfare of our family paid off in a big way. We were settled in our new home, attending church, and growing in the Lord. All was well for the moment, but that was not the end of the story. I made so many mistakes raising my sons, as all fathers do.

My mistake, believe it or not, centered around church. I loved my church, and I attended nearly every service. And we had services: Monday, Wednesday, Thursday, Friday, Saturday, and sometimes three times on Sunday we were in church. You would think that attending church was a good thing, and it really is, but too much church *can* and *will* affect the family. I missed out on opportunities to get my sons involved with sports or learning to play an instrument. So many moments that could have been but were missed because we were in church. While it was good that my sons grew up to love the Lord, there are things in life that children need to experience *apart* from church. They need to have balance in their lives. We cannot be short-sighted in the development or our children.

Raising children in any era is a difficult challenge. Raising them with the flawed values I had gained from my family issues made that challenge even more difficult. I come from a family of eight children, my mother and father fought (literally) on a regular basis, and all my siblings gave birth to children (or fathered, as in my brother's case) out of wedlock. I don't think any of us got our high school diplomas the traditional way. It's hard to remember when Christmas or birthday celebrations gave us a feeling of anticipation; with seven kids (my baby brother passed away of cerebral palsy at the age of six), our parents just couldn't afford to give us much.

When my parents separated and eventually divorced, she took the three youngest children, of which I am one, with the four oldest staying with my father. Although we struggled financially, there was a lot of love going around, even for my father and separated siblings. But would that be enough to get us through those challenging times? Only time would tell. It was not all bad, though. I learned how to survive, and how to be content with such things as I had. And although I still made mistakes raising my sons, I was determined not to make the ones my father made; I was not going to hit my wife, no matter how angry I got. That curse was going to end with me, and in 43 years, I never did. I wanted to leave a different legacy for my sons.

Thankfully, my sons learned from the mistakes I made. I am a proud grandfather of eight highly intelligent grandchildren. Coached by her dad, my oldest granddaughter Khayla played basketball for a local college and is now serving in the U.S. Navy. My oldest grandson Zion is an accomplished jazz drummer. Zachary is on the swim team, Jabari sings and plays the keyboard, and Antonio plays peewee football. We have yet to see what will become of the three younger grands, Malachi, Eli, and Savanah, but no doubt they will turn out fine.

The moral of the story is this: Sometimes, love *can* be enough! Love will make a man be there for his family. Love will cause him to deny himself so that his family has what they need. Love will make a man fight, defend, and even die for the protection of his family. So if all you have to offer your family is love, use it. Love can make up for all the mistakes you *will* make as a father, but you must allow your love to push you where you may fear to go. Parenting is challenging, even scary at times, but love will get you through it. Your mistakes do not define you; they remind you. They remind you of what you did wrong so you can avoid them in the future. Love your kids; be there for them, because sometimes love is all you have.

 **Jonathan Rudd, II** grew up in Columbia, Maryland, the second son of Pastor Jonathan Rudd and the late Prophet Helen S. Rudd. He has a brother, Stephon Rudd, who has recently started a podcast called, "ThePhonCast". Jonathan is currently operating a travel business with his wife Ingrid Rudd (J-I World Travel) and a credit and financial services business (ZDEBGLO).

After working 23 years at the National Cancer Institute as a GS-12 Contracting Officer, he is looking to finish two more years, and seeking early retirement from the Federal Government to write the next chapter of his life, doing full-time ministry and traveling the world, spreading the Gospel with his wife.

He is a proud father of three, a daughter who currently serves in the Navy, a son who just graduated high school, who writes music and sings, and a stepson who has just graduated Marine boot camp (Ooh Rah). In 2018, he and his wife bought their first house together and they have made it a home built on the foundation of God.

Jonathan has always admired his father for the book that he wrote, "Faith that Recovers All" and has always desired to become an author himself. Writing a chapter in this book is truly an honor and he hopes that this will be the beginning of something new and great for future writing endeavors.

Life Keeps Life-ing

Jonathan Rudd, II

• • • • • • • • • • • •

It's 5:35 a.m. I've finally found some time for peace and quiet. This is usually my quiet time to pray and meditate on God's word. In this moment, I will take time to share my story.

When I was first introduced to authoring a chapter in the Black Fathers' Perspective project, I was so excited because writing is something that I've always wanted to do. Here's my shot and from my experience as basketball coach, you miss 100% of the shots that you do not take. But then it occurred to me that I am not a writer, so do I pass the ball and try again later?

I reached out to my father for support and suggestions and just like always, he came up with a good idea. He told me, "As far as your writer's block, don't think like a writer. Rather, think like a dad telling what he went through raising kids."

So that's what I tasked myself to do. What my dad said sounded so simple but sometimes a simple answer is all we truly need in response to our difficult problems.

I was raised in a home with both parents and so my expectations of family were different. Mom and Dad stayed together. Mom and Dad raised a family together and I had placed those high expectations on myself to do the same. Being in a Christ-centered home, and having Godly parents as role models, this is something that I should definitely be able to keep up. But as you know,

"LIFE KEEPS LIFE-ING."

On August 15, 2000, the Lord blessed me with my first child, a daughter. All I could think of was all the wonderful things that my dad had done with me when I was a child and now I had my own to do the same thing, but even better. Holding her for the first time was such a joy but I also felt the pressure of being a parent for the first time.

The following year, 9/11 happened and my life would change yet again. My heart goes out to the lives lost on that day but to be honest when I heard the news all I could think of was getting back home to my daughter. *What's going on? Why is it happening? How do I protect my daughter?* were the questions going on in my head. Sure, I was concerned about the lives lost and if any more things were going to happen. Although things changed across the country, we survived.

Two years later, on July 9, 2003, the Lord blessed me with my son. But there were other changes going on in my life—not on the same scale as the events of 9/11, but to me it was just as tragic. Besides now having two more mouths to feed, the dynamics in my home would change.

My home was no longer happy even with the new bundle of joy. I had to work a second job, because the wife wanted to rest and stay home. Then when I got home, there was tension and friction between the wife and me. We had come to a crossroad in our relationship and we weren't sure if we were able to go forward together. So we took time and separated while we tried to figure it out.

How have we come to this point in our relationship? How can I continue to raise my son and my daughter without being physically in the home? This is not the example that I saw from Mom and Dad so what do I do now?

That short three-year separation would end and we would try again, only to get separated again, and eventually we would get divorced. Of course, I moved out of the home and moved back home with my parents, who were now living in Charles Town, WV.

Needless to say, I spent many days on the road. My day was getting up at 6:00am to drive to work. Work started at 7:00am and ended at 3:30pm. Then I'd have to leave work to go to Columbia, MD to pick up my daughter to drive her to Anne Arundel County for basketball practice. Ended practice around 8:30pm and then I'd have to drive my daughter back home. While there I'd see my son, maybe help him with his homework, if I even understood how to do it, and then I'd head back home to West Virginia.

That schedule would be every Monday and Wednesday. On Saturdays and Sundays there were basketball tournaments, church and somewhere squeezed in there was me time…. Maybe soon!

I'm tired just writing this but this was my life and eventually it would catch up to me. Nobody can keep going on like that but I was expected to by my kids, their mom and even myself. I would even find time for birthdays and special visits as often as I could, but it wasn't the same.

I must admit, I spent the majority of my time back and forth trying to fix my marriage. Their mother would tell me that I needed to spend more time with the kids and focus more on them. In my eyes, I thought that I was but maybe I could do more.

My daughter and I carried a strong bond through basketball. I mean I was her basketball coach and we spent 80% of our time playing basketball and going to basketball tournaments. My son was not really into basketball; although I coached him for two years, it just wasn't his thing. So I got him involved in Tae Kwon Do and football. Football was short-lived because he only went to one football practice and decided that it was not for him. I still have the pictures of him in his football gear though. Tae Kwon Do was hard for me to get him to practice since I had basketball practice with my daughter. I had no assistant coach and I had to be at practice, so my son ended up leaving Tae Kwon Do.

As time went on, there was a disconnect between my son and me but I was so blinded by my little good father deeds that I failed to see the problem. I was still hearing the praises from my mother, my father and others about how good a father I was and they only based this on the things that I was "doing" for them. There is another part to fatherhood that has nothing to do with the "doing" but has everything to do with "being."

Fast forward...

On July 8, 2016, I met the new love of my life, who would become the new Mrs. Rudd. We would marry in 2018 and purchase our first home the same year. I made sure to get four bedrooms. She already had a son and I was preparing two rooms for my son and daughter. By now, my relationship with my son had worsened. Being remarried didn't help and several times we clashed.

I would clash with my son. My son clashed with me. My wife would get upset and clash with him. Now I'm playing mediator between the two while still trying to keep peace in the home. Finally, I snapped.

My son and I got into it so heavily that we practically had a fistfight. I had him pinned against the wall. He didn't like it and head-butted me and loosened my tooth. I called the police in an attempt to strike fear. When they showed up a new fear came over me. What had I done?

This happened in the wake of multiple incidents of police brutality and police shooting black men like rabid dogs. Could this end up like one of those cases? Or would they arrest us both and then we were both screwed and tied up in a crooked system?

For the first time, I realized that I had to get a grip on this situation and see how we could have a better relationship... before he ended up dead.

You see, my son was a very angry young man. I am a firm believer that you may have two kids but you cannot discipline them the same way. I could talk to my daughter and she would listen. But my son... you could talk to him but he was going to have another word or comment behind it. I think it's the Rudd curse of always wanting to have the last word and always wanting to be right. My dad to this day still jokes and says, "I'm never wrong and the one time I thought I was wrong, I was actually right." It sounds funny, but I think my dad actually does live by this statement.

So one day I just decided to sit down with my son and talk. I don't mean that I did all of the talking and he just listened. I actually sat there and listened while he talked. I had to ask him, "Son, why are you so angry when I try to talk to you?" He responded that he came into the conversation expecting me to get angry so he attacked from the start.

I took time to listen to what he said before I responded. And to be honest, I could not get upset with what he said. In times past I may have been on edge and gotten upset right away and never really gave him time to express himself. Coming up, I never felt like I had the opportunity to express myself. It was whatever Dad says, that's it—no back talk. For the first time I saw myself and I did not like it. I was doing to my son the thing that I didn't like my dad doing to me: not allowing me to express myself without him getting angry.

So I promised my son that from now on he could speak and I would listen but I asked that he give me the same opportunity when I spoke. I told him, "You cannot come into every conversation expecting the worst because whatever you expect is what you will get. So if you come with a great expectation then the chances are you might have a great outcome or not. But at least give yourself a chance, give me a chance and most importantly, I'm sorry."

We further went on to discuss about his feelings in regard to me and his mother. I realized that some of the anger issues lay within that conversation. And just like I anticipated, he still had hopes that his mother and I would get back together again. In fact, he told me that he still hoped and was praying.

One of the things that I wish I had done when I separated from his mother was to sit down with both of my kids and their mother to express what was going on. I never had a chance to tell them that it wasn't their fault. I never got to tell them how we would make this work. Not that I felt like I had to, but I should have.

Later in the conversation my son would agree that even though he prayed that his mother and I would get back together, he realized that it was really for the best that we did not. He had seen the arguments we'd had with each other and he did not like it. It was not a healthy environment to try to raise kids in. Although I would never hit her, I would always get in my car and drive off. Maybe it might seem childish to some but I would rather have done that than be in jail for something that I should not have done. But I never really considered what it did to my son and my daughter.

Growing up in a Christian home with parents who stayed together, I've always felt badly about being divorced. I believe the biggest fear about divorcing was wondering how many of my Christian friends would feel about it.

Remember that comment that I made about being a father as opposed to doing things expected of a father? What I realized was that being a father has more to do with how I am toward my kids.

It doesn't matter about where they live as opposed to where I live. It has little to do with me actually spending physical time with them, although it is important when you can spend time with them to do so.

I reached out to a good friend, Lawrence Perry, for support because I wanted to establish a relationship with my son and my daughter but did not know how. Although my daughter stayed with me before she went to the Navy, my son still lived with his mother. The ideal way was to be with him physically but that could not always be. So he told me to not worry about it and just connect in any way that I could.

How did I want it to look? Well, I wanted to be married and have my kids live with me happily ever after. How does it actually look? I'm happily married but my kid lives with his mother. I cannot always drive up there to see him because it's a lot of hours on the road and wear and tear on my body.

When I call or text, he barely replies back to me or answers the phone. I want to hang out with him but he works and has school. So I did my best and connected with him anyway, in every way possible. I even made sure to always tell him that I love him. And one day he surprised me and said he loved me first.

Now that he has graduated high school, I drove up there with him to help him get his license. I let him use my car to drive to get the hours he needed behind the wheel. I taught him how to park and all the driving skills he needed to pass this test. I sat back and watched to see how excited he got when he did it correctly.

We still have our heart-to-heart conversations about life, what he sees in the world today and how he needs to respond. I still worry if he will become a statistic.

I just pray that he has enough in him to hold back his temper and let God speak through him and calm his temperament in those situations. When I tell my friends who are Caucasian about this situation they seem to not connect to this idea. They just think that it's only in our heads that this is happening. I can assure you that night I called the police on my son still haunts me to this day. When I get pulled over by the police I wonder if I will be a statistic.

I may not be the best father in the world to my kids but I learn from my mistakes so I can become better. There is no handbook on how to do this. Being a father requires you to be connected to your children and to hear them. After all, we do have two ears and one mouth. We are to hear twice as much before we speak. You never know, you could learn something about yourself through your son because they are listening.

When I coached basketball, I always gave the girls that I coached a life lesson. Life lessons that they can apply to basketball also apply to real life. So I did not have many issues with my daughter. But my son never got those moments. And for a moment I think he felt left out. We're still working on our relationship even though he's now 18 and about to become an adult in the world.

We will keep working on this relationship because after all…

"life keeps life-ing."

**Floyd Brown II,** is a Baltimore, Maryland native, Exhorter for Holy Manifestation Ministries in Northern Virginia. He is the Author of "A Deeper Place: Divine Vision for God's People." As a graduate of Calling & Ministry Studies (CAMS) Church of God Ministries in Roanoke, Virginia, he has facilitated various church functions as Elder and Council Member within Maryland, Delaware, and Virginia. Earning a Bachelor of Arts degree in Psychology at Ashford University in Clinton, Iowa he was able to actively study common dysfunctions within society that often obstruct phases of diversity. Floyd then studied Psychology further at the University of the Rockies in Denver, Colorado earning a Master of Arts degree. That was the moment when he perceived effective ways to mediate between cultures to find effective resolution strategies.

For personal and spiritual growth, his primary work within the last 20 years has involved the church community. That mission has been to help God's people discover their true purpose and calling within the body of Christ through foundations of encouragement and discipleship.

With dedicated service to God, Floyd is compelled to deliver spiritually inspired messages as a speaker, as well as provide godly counsel to those who will receive it.

The Minority Struggle of America

Floyd Brown II

• • • • • • • • • • • • •

INTRODUCTION

In an immensely diverse American society, there are numerous viewpoints and lifestyles for one to consider. There are a variety of experiences, situations, and teachings people encounter within their distinct backgrounds. As a result of those dissimilarities, one's sense of wisdom, social standing, and character varies (LeBaron, 2003). In many cases, immoral living standards often mislead people into unhealthy lifestyles and behaviors. Even though some people tend to live productive lives, they still may not have identified with their true sense of worth and purpose. The most important phase of life is the interconnection between mankind and divine purpose through God. As we teach our children the demands of life, it is equally essential to pronounce the value they bring to society through determination and reverence to the creator. Identifying with one's true purpose in God is essential for living healthy and meaningful lifestyles, even in the face of apparent challenges.

· · · · · ·

Today is another moment in history that is not so kind to minorities in America. And as we know this concern has intensified over the last few years. Hatred and racism have seared through America. Blacks, Middle Easterners, Hispanics, and now Asians are all being oppressed in some way. But one of the greatest misconceptions of our society is to believe that all White individuals are hard workers, all Blacks are criminals, all Middle Easterners are terrorists, all Hispanics are abusers of the immigration system, and that all Asians eat exotic foods that are harmful. However, the fact is that not all cultural groups share the same moral fortitude or personal interests. You will find the good and the bad in each community. For example, even within the police culture itself, there are honorable acts of extreme heroism as well as various acts of dishonor and disgrace. Each culture and each community has its attributes as well as its flaws. There are some people who will sometimes fit into stereotypes. Yet, there are often others that do not fit into a specific character trait or lifestyle that society tends to put them into.

The America that I always believed in and served in the military to fight for has sometimes not fought enough for me - a black man. I say that because as a former U.S. Marine and law enforcement officer, I too have faced issues of racism whenever the uniform was not worn. I have walked into stores and often been followed and stared at as if I did something wrong. However, the people subtly harassing me in those moments had no idea that I am the very person who would unselfishly defend them if they were in need. There were numerous encounters when I walked by a woman of diverse ethnicity, and they clenched their purse as if I was a thief. Even while driving I have been profiled by police officers just because I drove through a predominantly white neighborhood. After noticing me, the police officer abruptly turned his vehicle around and followed me while he most likely ran my tags. But after approximately two miles driving behind me, he eventually discontinued his approach and drove in another direction. But these are the things that were always of huge discussion within the black communities and have recently increased in conversation: concerns about how to react, how to cope, how to assimilate into America.

WHERE DO I FIT IN?

In a society where each person has their purpose, where do I fit in?

As a minority, I am looked upon as ill-fated, misjudged by the color of my skin, hated by those who think of me as being inferior to them. Yet I breathe and bleed the same way they do. Will I ever be fully accepted?

Where do I fit in?

As a former law enforcement officer, I have been depicted by society as someone who stirs up strife because of the declaration of my uniform – as if I would seek to harm or blatantly diminish those I come in contact with – due to the bad choices some of my fellow officers have made. Yet I was merely there to protect and serve – to actually make a difference.

Where do I fit in?

As an employee, I was surrounded by co-workers who voted for a former president who did not value moral stability and decency in our society, a president filled with hatred, pride, greed, arrogance, and who often advocated violence. With no hesitation he would shockingly say anything out of his mouth. Yet children are watching, people are hurting, and hatred is still stirring today.

Where do I fit in?

As a U.S. Marine, I have always been portrayed in the civilian world as being half-deranged, hostile, and intimidating. Yes, I did learn to be aggressive and I have seen some crazy things that I ultimately survived. But the training I partook in does not fully define who I am. I am a person who genuinely cares for others, who defends those who need support. Yet I am hated in the Middle East by those I would unselfishly preserve.

Where do I fit in?

As a minister, I am identified as a servant of God who seeks holiness and restoration in the churches. I come from a breed that does not believe in church as usual, sitting idle, and leaving church the same way I came in. I believe in the power of the Holy Ghost and the movement of God as each spirit-filled member has a voice to pronounce the undeniable glory of God. When will some churches come out of their sense of complacency?

Where do I fit in?

I will just fit in where God's heart leads and do the best I can to follow it.

I will fit in…

Nevertheless, to fit in, I must find a way to assimilate into society. You see, culturally I am mixed-race, but I am also Black. Being Black in America (or any country) does not make me a criminal; that's not me. Being Black does not make me lazy, because I'm not. Being Black does not make me a person who likes drama and confusion, because I don't. But being Black only means that God has chosen me to be one of His many varieties to choose from. God has created a variety of things. Not every ocean has the same depth. Trees do not all measure the same height, nor do they all appear the same. The animals we all know are even distinct in their appearance. But they all serve their purposes. As humans we typically don't even eat the same foods every day and we don't usually wear the exact same clothes each year. Nor are our days always the same. But there is wisdom and understanding given to us as our life experiences remain unique and diverse. God uses diversity not for mankind to search for flaws in one another; He uses diversity to emphasize the beauty and the artistry He has designed for Himself in every one of us. It is not the distinction of a person that matters, but it is the HEART of a person that is of substance. If it is a heart that seeks to preserve peace between others, then it is productive.

The Bible says, "Man looks on the OUTWARD appearance, but the LORD looks on the HEART" 1 Samuel 16:7, ESV

One of the greatest aspects of being a father of any culture is demonstrating to your children what good character really means. It is embodied in holding true to the right values for them to follow, instilling in them the significance of treating others with dignity, respecting their elders, being at peace with others, believing in themselves when others don't, refraining from negative influence, and actively acknowledging God, which are all essential characteristics of good parenting. The Bible says, "Train up a child in the way he should go: and when he is old, he will not depart from it." Prov. 22:6, KJV. And it is just as important to also tell our children the truth about the apparent troubles happening within our society. For instance, if we speak of only the good, they will not be prepared for the bad things that may come their way. It's sort of like driving a vehicle. We are not only urged to learn how to drive proficiently enough to avoid making mistakes, we are also urged to drive defensively by preparing for the mistakes of others. Therefore, we must impart to our children the most significant information possible and provide the best course of direction that will guide them when we are eventually no longer around.

As a Black male, I often teach my children all the positive things to hope for in life. But I likewise inform them of all the unfortunate challenges that Blacks face in America. I feel obligated to tell them how Black people seem to not acquire the same level of justice other nationalities receive. As uncomfortable as it is, I explain how intense hatred can be in America and how best to avoid these conflicts. And as a Black father in America, I will still continue to teach all of my five children to treat others as themselves and to perceive the content of character over the color of skin, to give respect to authority and to eagerly find ways to bridge the gap between various cultural groups. Of course, it is a continuous struggle assimilating into a society that too often values personal agenda and privilege over humanity. But choosing to forgive and accept others in our lives regardless of differences is part of the undertaking God has given to us all.

1 Peter 3:8 says, "Finally, be ye ALL of ONE MIND, having COMPASSION one of another, LOVE as BRETHREN, be MERCIFUL, be COURTEOUS."

And we must keep in mind that God has formed us all for His own purposes. One essential aspect we all have in common is that we deserve to keep the breath in our bodies that God has given us. We were all made by the hand of God—our souls are the same color and our skin colors are God's variety. He breathed life into each one of us to establish a purpose here on the earth (Gen.2:7). And that breath that runs through our bodies belongs to God - not to be taken away by another. And by now, we should all realize that criminals come in all colors, just as law-abiding citizens do.

For that reason, we have no right to discriminate against or to mistreat another person based on their cultural background. In other words, we must not criticize, condemn, or hold responsible one community for the careless disassociation of one person. Not all people are identical in nature... These are the things we must share with our children. Without a doubt, we must find ways to better understand one another. An effective strategy for bridging the gap between people is to attentively listen, discover similarities, and then build relationships from those efforts. Because if we fail to listen to those who are expressing their personal concerns, mistreatments, and struggles, we will always be divided. And this is not what we want for our children – a divided society. Therefore, the most important question is how much do we want to understand one another? Do we really listen to others? Are we sensitive enough to see that someone else has encountered something different than we have?

Even though unjust and discriminatory situations happen, I will always love every nationality. What others depict me as does not define me. God defines me. How someone depicts you will not change how God feels about you. The problems we face don't take away the purposes God has for us. God does not show partiality with skin color. But he does see oppression. And every so often, He exposes injustice for it to be seen. Regardless of those difficulties, He has always shown through our distinctions that He is a God who favors variety and desires inclusion for each culture. The will of God has been set forth as a journal within the scriptures on how we are to relate to others and emulate His character. It is not our position to withhold the rights of others based on our own desires. But God has promoted and will always promote equality, peace, and decency in the midst of all people. It is written to love thy neighbor as thyself.

Leviticus 19:18 says – "Thou shalt NOT AVENGE, nor bear ANY GRUDGE against the children of thy people, but thou shalt LOVE THY NEIGHBOR as THYSELF: I AM the LORD."

So, brothers and Sisters of all ethnicities, let us continue to please the Lord by avoiding hate and division - refraining from all forms of unruliness and deception. Hold fast to what is good, holy, pure, and true (1 Thessalonians 5:21, Philippians 4:8, John 8:32). Be aware of behaviors and actions that may defile us. Ensure that the perspective of our hearts and minds are not contrary to the truth of God's Word. Line up the scriptures with the character and moral standing of Jesus - which is the foundation of true redemption and salvation. Teaching our children to be at peace with all mankind and to find constructive ways to resolve conflict can save lives. Approaching things the right way can mean the difference between life and death (spiritually and physically).

Matthew 5:44, NIV says, "But I tell you, LOVE your ENEMIES and PRAY for those who PERSECUTE YOU."

Hebrews 12:14, NLT also says, "Work at LIVING in PEACE with EVERYONE, and work at LIVING a HOLY LIFE, for those who are NOT HOLY will NOT see the LORD."

GOD HAS A PLAN

It is a highly honorable gesture to genuinely seek unity between others instead of tearing each other down based on the variances of our backgrounds. We should all be one unified America, an America that best describes the right path for our children to emulate so that perhaps they may realize doing good has its rewards and that God ultimately has a plan if we only submit ourselves to it.

John 13:35, NLT says, "YOUR LOVE for ONE ANOTHER will PROVE to the WORLD that YOU are MY DISCIPLES."

Loving others does not mean condoning one's behavior or agreeing with their decisions. It essentially means you choose to do the right thing - to love them and pray for them despite their offenses. For instance, if someone tells you that you did not do something properly, it does not mean they are your enemy. It only means they are bringing a sense of awareness to you. To put it differently, if someone is different in the way they approach life, it does not mean they are necessarily your enemy. In such cases, they might just need a clearer sense of understanding in order to relate well with your own belief system. Likewise, in reference to church practices, if someone speaks the truth to you or warns you of unholy actions as a form of correction, it does not mean they don't love you. It actually means they do love you enough to bring the truth. As God's creation, we are called to expose the truth in love and to encourage aspects of unity so that others may comprehend a better way. Avoiding falsehood and speaking truth to what's unjust is the foundation of what God Himself declares. We must hold true to the truth by preserving upright behavior and adhering to the holiness God has laid out for us since the beginning. Even within some of our religious institutions we will encounter some challenges. Nevertheless, we must understand that we are not identical; we are varied in many ways. Yet, if God has called us all to encourage one another and help build His Kingdom, why not work together? Of course, our approaches will not be the same, but our goals are usually the same. That mission is to patiently love one another and bring glory to the Lord - working cohesively as God intended us to.

Ephesians 5:27, KJV says, "That HE might present it to HIMSELF a GLORIOUS CHURCH, NOT having SPOT, or WRINKLE, or any such thing; but that it should be HOLY and WITHOUT BLEMISH."

In fact, God has created men and women of God to uniquely serve within the Body of Christ. Not all people talk the same, not all teachers teach alike, not all people pray quietly, not all ministers preach in the same way. In fact, not all people show love the same way. But their approach to showing kindness may be demonstrated in other ways. One person's heart may not be as mushy as yours; but it doesn't mean they haven't displayed love. Therefore, people do not all have the same uses, traits, or the same way of doing things. The way we interact, express our thoughts, and deliver messages can often vary. For example, the way one pours their heart out for God may be different than the way you pour your heart out for God. Your participation within the church may be different than the way God has someone else participate. Understanding that each person is unique is essential to social and personal growth. In the same way, our children will need to identify with those possibilities in life despite their hardships—to somehow develop methods of interaction that mediate relationships among people inside and outside the church. They must also come to realize that not everyone will accept them, but to ultimately strive to live meaningful lives. Even though we are all unique and often encounter conflicts between people, God has a significant purpose for our existence. There are a variety of ways in which God emphasizes the purposes of humanity—through distinct gifts, talents, and efforts of participation. This involvement is to encourage one another within the capacity He has given us. And as communities of diverse nations, we must adamantly pursue a sense of unity regardless of unwarranted encounters concerning social injustice. In light of the great number of distinctions between us all, there is still hope.

Romans 12:4, NIV says, "For just as each of us has one body with many members, and these members do NOT all have the SAME FUNCTION."

Ephesians 4:16, NIV says, "From HIM the whole body, JOINED and HELD TOGETHER by every supporting ligament, GROWS and BUILDS ITSELF UP in love, as each part does its work."

In fact, with some level of determination, we can help build our communities to stimulate substantial measures of social reform, justice, stability, and godly living. But each person must do their part so that God can freely do His part through us. There is an assignment God has placed in your hands… And if you only adhere to it, you will discover the true essence of your existence.

Unity is PARAMOUNT for any civilization. And whether we have similar backgrounds and cultures or not, we are still capable of passing on encouragement and inspiration in the spirit of unity – extending kindness to the next person. In this way, we not only please God, but we make a positive impact on society and our children.

1 Corinthians 1:10, NIV says, "I appeal to you, brothers and sisters, in the name of our Lord Jesus Christ, that all of you AGREE with ONE ANOTHER in what you say and that there be NO DIVISIONS AMONG YOU, but that you be PERFECTLY UNITED in MIND and THOUGHT."

"Therefore, let us NOT PASS JUDGEMENT on ONE ANOTHER ANY LONGER, but rather decide NEVER to put a STUMBLING

BLOCK or HINDRANCE In the way of a BROTHER." Romans 14:13, ESV

Let us support one another in unity and continue to accept the diversity of all nations. Pray that we accomplish or solidify a substantial measure of change that reduces the challenges associated with cultural diversity. Ask God with heartfelt desperation to provide wise counsel and guidance to our American leaders so they may perhaps consider THE HEART OF GOD INSTEAD OF THEIR OWN. Keep hope alive for our nation—pray that it will recognize true justice, diversity, and social and economic equality. Value genuine unity and forgiveness—recognize the dramatic impact it has between cultures. Discover and preserve your God-given purpose within the body of Christ. Let holiness, reaching out to those in need, and pursuing the OUTPOURING of God's Spirit be your way of life. After this COVID season ends, go to your local churches yearning and expecting a special presence from the Lord the way God's people did on the day of Pentecost. If not, find the undeniable presence of God right where you are—He will find you. And despite our socio-economic challenges in America today, let us teach our children godly principles and give them the tools needed to resolve conflicts that will cohesively build thriving communities. By allowing God to do HIS WORK in them and THROUGH them, they can effectively assimilate into their environments to perhaps divert the blinded course of dissonance and division in society.

In The Spirit of Unity,

F. Brown II

About the Visionary Author

Kimmoly K. LaBoo is a Published Author, International Speaker and Certified Master Life Coach. She is at the helm of LaBoo Publishing Enterprise, as CEO and founder. She is a highly respected change agent in her community and around the world.

Her award-winning company was created for the independent self-publisher. Kimmoly enjoys providing expert guidance and unlimited support to her clients, helping them recognize their brilliance, sharing their stories with the world, as writers.

She has dedicated her life to serving girls and women through mentoring, and coaching. Her compassionate coaching style, challenges clients to embrace change and show up confidently, using their unique gifts and talents to impact and serve others.

She has been named among the Top 25 Women in Business by Courageous Woman magazine. She has appeared on Think Tech Hawaii, WPB Networks, Heaven 600, ABC2News, FOX5 News, WMAR2 News, and has graced many stages speaking and training to include, Department of Veterans Affairs, Blacks in Government National Training Conference, and Coppin State University.

Kimmoly is the mother of two amazing sons and currently resides in Maryland.

Contact Information:
www.laboopublishing.com
staff@laboopubishing.com

Suggested Reading

Black fathers play a pivotal role in the lives of our black children. According to the 2011 U.S. Census, nearly 2 in 3 (64%) African American children live in father-absent homes. However, we know all fathers are not absent. Society would have us to believe that black fathers are either in jail, or on drugs and are no good to the community.

The Black Father Perspective is a collaboration of men who have come together to give voice to a population that is often overlooked and underappreciated. It is time to change the narrative. It is time to shift the agenda. Ten black fathers share their view on legacy, marriage, divorce, single parenting, teenage parenting, incarceration, child support and so much more. Reading this book will give you a new perspective of Black Fathers in America. This is what they want you to know.

www.ingramcontent.com/pod-product-compliance
Lightning Source LLC
Chambersburg PA
CBHW071757040426
42446CB00012B/2600